In-Laws

RESOURCES FOR BIBLICAL LIVING

In-Laws

Married with Parents

WAYNE A. MACK

P&R
PUBLISHING
P.O. BOX 817 • PHILLIPSBURG • NEW JERSEY 08865-0817

Some of the material in this booklet has been adapted from Wayne A. Mack and Carol Mack, Sweethearts for a Lifetime (Phillipsburg, NJ: P&R Publishing, 2006). I also want to acknowledge and express my gratitude to Deborah Howard, whose editorial skills helped shape this booklet, and to Lou Priolo, who invited me to participate in this series and then provided appendix 6 as a valuable asset to this booklet's usefulness.

Printed in the United States of America

ISBN: 978-1-59638-170-4

HOW MANY CHRISTIAN BOOKS about marriage would you say you have purchased and read? How many of them included solid biblical teaching, if any teaching, about the issue of in-law relationships? Over the years I have purchased and read hundreds of books on marriage and family issues. Surprisingly, a perusal of these books indicates that very little has been written on this subject. It's virtually an untouched area.

The truth is that this subject, in general, is largely neglected, and specific teaching on in-law difficulties from a biblical perspective is rare, indeed. On the numerous occasions when I have taught on this problem from a biblical perspective, I have had people tell me, time and again, that they had never heard, read, or even thought about a biblical approach to godly in-law relations. Yet, after counseling hundreds of troubled marriages during the past forty years or so, I have become increasingly convinced that in-law relationships pose serious problems to many marriages.

While doing a web search on the subject of in-law relationships, I came across a number of articles (written by experts on marriage and family issues according to the world) that discussed the relationship between in-law relations and success in a marriage. *All* of these articles agreed that in-law relations can cause serious problems in a marriage relationship. For example, one article reported the results of a study done in 2001 by Iowa University that assessed the connection between in-law relations and the future success of marriage. The researchers examined all four of the in-law relationships individually.

From this study the researchers drew many insightful conclusions. One was that each of the in-law combinations, not just the mother-in-law relationship as is sometimes assumed, played a significant role in the marriage. Fathers-in-law can affect the quality of a marriage just as much as mothers-in-law. Interestingly, the investigation also revealed that in-law relations can create problems not just for the recently married, but also for people who have been married for a long time. They found that in-laws can create hostility and stress between spouses even after many years of marriage. This, they noted, is significant because "it implies that the influence of in-laws continues far beyond the early years of marriage, when couples are probably most vulnerable to social influences on their marriage. Perhaps," they concluded, "that vulnerability to the opinions and behaviors of those who are close to them *never ends.*"[1]

Since non-Christians probably conducted this research, the likelihood exists that most of the people being surveyed were also non-Christians. Therefore, the ultimate reliability of the results of such a study is somewhat suspect for Christians. We would certainly hope and expect that the percentage of Christians who are having serious in-law problems would be much lower than that of unbelievers. But those of us who are involved in biblical marriage counseling will freely admit that this can be a serious problem for Christians and non-Christians alike.

Biblical Examples of In-Law Problems

It shouldn't surprise us that this is so. This is not a new thing! When we turn to the Bible we see frequent examples of God's people struggling with in-law relationships.

In the book of Genesis, we find that Isaac and Rebekah, for example, had some problems with the wives of Esau. The Bible

---

1. Gina Stepp, "The Effect of In-Laws on Marriage Success," *Family Matters*, December 20, 2007, http://familymatters.vision.org/public/item/192944 (emphasis added).

says they brought much grief to their hearts (Gen. 26:34–35). The Bible tells us of the in-law problem that Jacob had with Laban, his father-in-law. In Genesis 31 they parted company— it was not a very happy parting. Jacob went one way and Laban went the other. You no doubt remember that "nice" benediction where Laban says, "LORD watch between me and thee when we are absent one from another" (Gen. 31:49 KJV). And we say, "Wasn't that lovely?" Not when you consider that what Laban was really saying was, "You'd better not ever come back here again because if you do the only deliverance you are going to have is from God." He didn't like his son-in-law and it appears the favor was returned. So they agreed to part ways. As far as we know, they never got back together again.

The book of Judges reveals that mighty Samson also had in-law problems (Judg. 15:1–8). King David had in-law problems. His own father-in-law wanted to kill him, and seeking some way to destroy him, chased him for years (1 Sam. 18:20–30). So it shouldn't surprise us that God's people still have in-law problems because they are present very early in the biblical account.

Hope for You and Those You Love

Maybe you're presently facing tensions with in-law relationships. Whatever your problems are in this area, I pray that perhaps something you'll read here today will prove helpful in solving your specific in-law problems. Maybe you are aware of these problems in the lives of a friend or a family member. I pray that you might find helpful information here with which you may minister to that troubled one in your life. The Bible says, "You who are spiritual restore such a one in a spirit of gentleness, considering yourself lest you also be tempted. Bear one another's burdens, and so fulfill the law of Christ" (Gal. 6:1–2 NKJV). As Christians, we bear a responsibility to help other people.

Perhaps you have no problems of this sort at this time, but you anticipate one day becoming a husband or wife who will then have the privilege and the responsibility of a godly relationship with your spouse's family. Maybe you're married with young children. Someday those children will bring someone new into your family and it will then be your duty to share a godly relationship with that person. I pray this booklet will help prepare you for that relationship.

It's still a fact that most people in America and even in the world do get married at some point, which means almost everyone is going to be an in-law. It's also a fact that when people get married they bring their family into the relationship too, which multiplies the probability and complexity of problems. Think of the problems found within only one family! It's no wonder that when families unite, problems multiply! For a young, married couple, that's a lot to have dumped on you at one time.

Thus, we have a need for such a booklet as this one. In these pages, I will assert practical suggestions and biblical doctrines that can guide you through this quagmire of possible relational difficulties and, through the grace of God, can help you navigate these sticky situations in a godly, respectful manner.

The Marriage Relationship Comes First

Before delving into the area of in-law relationships, let's review God's blueprint for marriage. Second Timothy 3:16–17 says, "All Scripture is inspired by God and profitable for teaching, for reproof, for correction, for training in righteousness; so that the man of God may be adequate, equipped for every good work." One such good work God desires to equip us for is that of being the kind of husband or wife to our spouse that He has designed us to be. That equipping, as Paul points out, takes place through the Scripture—through studying, understanding, and applying the Word of God to our lives. God's blueprint for marriage is revealed in His Word, and part of that blueprint involves being committed to the priority of the marriage relationship. Simply stated, the bond with our husband or wife is to be the most important human relationship in our lives!

The book of Ephesians provides a good representation of the order of importance our relationships should take. Chapters 1 through 3 talk about our highest priority—our relationship with the Lord. In chapters 4 through 6, Paul explains how we should relate to the different people in our life. After giving some general principles for interpersonal relationships in chapter 4 and the beginning of chapter 5, Paul gets very specific about the most important relationships. Starting in Ephesians 5:22, he gives some critical guidelines for the husband-wife relationship. This is followed by commands for the parent-child relationship (6:1–4) and then, finally, relationships between employees and employers in the workplace (6:5–9).

Paul uses this deliberate ordering to emphasize that the most important human relationship we have is with our mate. After God, marriage is first, children are second, and work is third. We know that this order is deliberate because Paul repeats it (almost verbatim in the books of Colossians and 1 Timothy). In 1 Timothy, he includes this ordering in the qualifications for church leadership. He begins by writing, "An overseer, then, must be above reproach, the husband of one wife" (1 Tim. 3:2). In verse 4, he mentions children, and finally, in verses 6–7, he talks about relationships with other people.

When Paul wrote "the husband of one wife," he was not primarily talking about being monogamous or not being divorced. One of the facts Paul is emphasizing, by including this in the context of church leadership qualifications, is that men who desire leadership roles are to be to their wives everything that God desires them to be because they will be examples to other men in the church. How they love, lead, and serve their wives will be observed by others, and therefore they must be above reproach. Pastors and elders do not just verbalize the Word of God—they *live* it!

This passage indicates that if a man is not relating properly to his wife, he has no business being part of the teaching and leading ministry of the church. This is important because it shows us how important the marriage relationship is. It is not that Paul is holding pastors and elders to a higher standard of conduct than other men in the church, but rather he is pointing out to all men how supremely important their relationship to their wives should be. Because it is so important, pastors and elders should be visible examples for the church in this matter.

Other passages in Scripture refer to the supremacy of the marriage relationship as well. In Titus 2:4, Paul says that older, godly women should "encourage the young women to love their husbands, to love their children. . . ." Again, the marriage relationship comes first. In Genesis 2:24, God establishes marriage and says, "For this reason a man shall leave his father and his mother, and be joined to his wife; and they shall become one flesh."

The One-Flesh Concept

Parents and their married children need to understand the meaning and implications of the statement "the two shall become one flesh" if they are to understand God's plan for parent-child relationships after the children get married. When rightly understood, this assertion makes it clear that the husband-wife relationship takes precedence over the parent-child relationship. Nowhere in Scripture is it stated that parents and children are to become one flesh. This declaration that in marriage the two become one flesh establishes the fact that as far as God is concerned there is something uniquely different about the marriage relationship that makes it more important in the overall picture of life than any other human relationship—even the parent-child relationship. Of this relationship God says that the two are joined (glued, welded) together and that no man should put this relationship asunder (Matt. 19:5–6). Nowhere does the Scripture make any statement similar to this one about the parent-child relationship.

Biblically defined this oneness consists in *a life long, exclusive, comprehensive union of an entire man and an entire woman to each other*. It certainly means that a husband and wife are to have a relationship with each other that they share with no one else other than their mate. It means they are to have a comprehensive partnership in *every area of life*. *It means that they are to be lastingly united to one another as long as they are both alive.* In other words, God's plan would never allow one spouse to say to the other, "That's none of your business," and that is to be true as long as they both shall live. Being one flesh means that the wife has complete, unfettered access to every area of her husband's life and so also the husband to every area of his wife's life. It means that there can't be any locked closets or hidden secrets in their marriage. That in essence is what it means to be "one flesh," *and nowhere does the Scripture describe any other human relationship in this way. And that has implications for parent-child relationships after marriage.*

Leaving Father and Mother

In his book, *Solving Marriage Problems*, Jay Adams wrote, "Perhaps the most difficult of all relationships to deal with is the in-law relationship. It is true that you marry the family. Unlike other situations, you cannot simply avoid your in-laws."[2] God, the Author of marriage, anticipated this difficulty. He knew that the matter of leaving father and mother would be difficult and

2. Jay E. Adams, *Solving Marriage Problems: Biblical Solutions for Christian Counselors* (Phillipsburg, NJ: P&R Publishing, 1983), 68.

so He included a command regarding this aspect of marriage in His very first statement on the subject.

I believe that most of us do not truly comprehend what leaving mother and father entails. In my experience as a counselor, I have found that, though many people would deny that they have any problems in this area, the matter of leaving is one of the most significant and problematic issues in marriage relationships. The idea of leaving father and mother is a broad concept that involves far more than most people realize. Before we discuss what leaving *does* mean, let me point out two things that leaving does *not* mean.

First, leaving father and mother does not mean that adult children stop honoring their parents. There is no time qualification in the fifth commandment. It does not mean that married children should stop listening to or welcoming and receiving counsel from their parents either. Proverbs 23:22 warns against this: "Listen to your father who begot you, and do not despise your mother when she is old." And, in Mark 7, Jesus rebuked the Pharisees for finding ways to avoid honoring or caring for their parents. First Timothy 5:8 gives one of the strongest warnings to believers: "If anyone does not provide for his relatives, and especially for his immediate family, he has denied the faith and is worse than an unbeliever" (NIV).

Second, leaving father and mother does not simply mean moving out of the parents' house. Children can move thousands of miles away from their parents and still not have really left them as God intended. In fact, parents may even be deceased, and their children have not really left them. After preaching on this subject some time ago, I was approached by a sixty-five-year-old man who had been married to his wife for forty years. He said to me, "I understand now why my wife and I have had so many problems in our relationship. My wife has never really left her mother and father." Though his wife's parents were long dead, the fact that she had never truly left them was still causing problems in their marriage. In my years of counseling, I have encountered this problem many times.

What leaving *does* mean is that there are certain aspects of the parent-child relationship before marriage that have to be put off after marriage. (The concepts of putting on and putting off will be explained in the next section.) This applies to parents and children alike. Some of these things are fairly obvious and some are not. At the same time, certain other things must be put on in terms of the parent-child relationship after marriage. It is vitally important, therefore, for the sake of attaining and maintaining a godly marriage relationship, that young couples (the ones who are leaving) and older couples (the ones who are letting them leave) rightly understand this concept of leaving father and mother.

Leaving Involves Putting Off

Children must leave behind an inordinate dependency on their parents when they get married. All children have a legitimate and appropriate dependence on their parents while growing up. Babies can do virtually nothing for themselves and depend on their parents for everything. When children are very young, they spend most of their day either eating or sleeping, but they cannot get themselves into bed or get food for themselves. They depend on their parents to change their diapers, bathe them, provide their food, and feed it to them. But as children get older, they learn to do more and more things for themselves and become less dependent. When people get married, they are to leave that kind of dependence behind.

A woman once told my wife that, even though her mother was dead, she still thought constantly about what her mother would say or do in certain situations. When she went shopping, she would think about whether or not her mother would approve of what she had bought. If she thought that her mother would not approve of some behavior, she usually would not do it. If she did it anyway, she would feel very guilty about it. That type of life is parent-centered and demonstrates that this woman had never really left her mother.

Children must put off the natural, imitative, or reactionary relationship that they have with their parents. In other words, they should not automatically do things the same way that their parents did just because that is what they are used to seeing their mothers and fathers do. On the other hand, they must not automatically do things differently just to be different. I have met people who have said things like, "My parents always made me go to Sunday school and I hated it, so I'm not making my kids go." Not liking something that their parents made them do is not, in itself, a valid reason for not doing it.

This means that adult married children must be prepared to examine the things their parents do to see whether they are biblical and to determine whether they are pleasing to God and beneficial for their family. Is it commanded in Scripture or is it merely a preference issue? Is it really what God indicates is best for the family or just something I want to do? These are questions that should be asked and carefully answered. Doing something or not doing something simply because it is the way their parents always did it is not a legitimate reason and does not demonstrate proper leaving of father and mother as God commanded.

Children must put off an inordinate reliance on their parents' approval. People must not base their own sense of security and happiness in life on their parents' opinions. Some people, even as adults, are devastated if their parents do not agree with them or approve of what they are doing.

In a similar vein, leaving their parents means that married people should be more concerned with fulfilling their *mate's* desires than their *parents'* desires. Scripture says that when a man gets married it is right and normal for him to be concerned about how to please his wife. Likewise, it asserts that it is right and normal for a woman who is married to focus on pleasing her husband (1 Cor. 7:32–34). At all times, pleasing God should be the first concern of every believer whether married or unmarried (2 Cor. 5:9), but after that, or perhaps as part of pleasing God, it would be proper for husbands and wives to make it a priority to please their mates even more than pleasing their mother or father or any other human being. In violation of this principle, I have heard a number of women say things like, "If his mother wants him to do something, he goes right over and does it, but if I need something done, forget it." Being more concerned with what our parents think and need than with what our mate thinks or needs is not leaving father and mother as God intended.

Children must put off a close and exclusive confidence with parents. In other words, their parents should not be the primary ones with whom they share all their secrets anymore. Many, many times in my counseling experience I have encountered situations in which the wife shares everything with her mother—any little difficulty with her husband, anything he did or did not do that she thought he should or shouldn't have done—and then wonders why her mother has such a bad opinion of her husband. I am sure that there are men who have this problem as well, but this aspect of leaving parents seems to be more problematic with women. People who do not cultivate one-flesh intimacy with their spouses have not truly left father and mother as God has commanded.

Children must be willing to give up their traditions regarding family structure and function, if Scripture does not command those traditions. For example, my wife and I were raised in very different types of families. I grew up on a farm with parents who had very little education. My wife's parents were very well educated (her father was a lawyer and a professor of law) and their family structure was quite different from mine. When we got married, we discovered that, though both our fathers had been the heads of their homes, the different ways in which our fathers exercised their leadership informed our individual ideas of headship and submission in the family.

From the beginning, we both agreed that God's biblical command was that I should be the head of the home and that He intended Carol to place herself in submission to me. Without knowing it, however, our definitions of leading and submitting had been influenced not only by Scripture, but also by the ways that our parents did things. Over time, we came to see that not all of our ideas were as biblical as we first thought them to be. This required us to carefully reexamine our family structure—how we related to each other, how we raised our children, how we made decisions, how we handled conflicts, how we communicated, how we spent our money, etc.—in light of God's Word.

Even something as seemingly minor as vacations was something we had to work through together. Until I was married, I never took a vacation in my life. Farm families worked during most days of the year. We took a little time off on Christmas morning, but then we went back to work. In Carol's family, vacation was a family ritual. Because her father taught law school for many years, they often spent their summers in the Pocono Mountains. While her father taught a law review course there, the rest of the family enjoyed a relaxing vacation. As a result, her perspective on taking time off was much different from mine. When we went on vacations together, my suitcase was full of books. To me, it just seemed wrong to relax and enjoy spending time with my family because all I knew from my childhood was work. We had to work through this and many other areas of family structure to determine what we were going to do in our family based on the Word of God, not on what our parents did.

Children must put off the tendency to play the blame game (Gen. 3:9–14). As long as people blame parents for their deficiencies—not enough love, encouragement, opportunities, material goods, etc.—they are not leaving them as God intended but remain attached. Harboring bitterness or resentment toward parents (playing the blame game) ties a person to parents in the same way that overspending with credit ties a person to the credit card company. A person in debt is not a free person, but is under constraint. Only when the debt is completely absolved is a person's mind and life free to function without the burden of debt constantly plaguing him. That's what happens when people stop playing the blame game with their parents.

When people stop blaming and condemning they leave behind all the bitterness and resentment they have carried with them from their childhood. When they recognize that no parent is perfect in the way they live or raise their children and are willing to be tenderhearted and forgiving as Christ commands, they experience freedom. Holding on to anger and resentment toward parents creates a negative bond that doesn't permit leaving as God intended and instead brings personal and familial destruction into marriage.

Leaving Involves Putting On

In the Bible, change is always a two-step process. It always involves putting some things off and other things on. When we are saved, the Bible teaches us that for real change to occur we must put off the ways of the flesh and put on Christlike qualities (Eph. 4:17–32; Col. 3:5–14). In terms of biblical parent-child relations after marriage, leaving involves putting off the practices we have just discussed, but it also means putting on certain new practices.

Children must put on a peer or friendship relationship with their parents. The relationship of dependency that people had with their parents as children must be replaced with a peer relationship. As people mature and develop a friendship with their parents, they begin to contribute to the lives of their parents as well as continue to benefit from their parents.

For example, our youngest son was a pastor in the United States for a number of years and is now a pastor/missionary in South Africa along with us. In both places we spend much time with him and his family and share in Christian ministry. Often when he has a big decision to make he and his wife will come to us and ask for our counsel. And in most cases, when we have major decisions to make, we turn to him (and our other children) for input and insight. We ask him and his wife to pray for us and seek their wisdom as we make decisions. We respect him greatly and have received much benefit from him as he presents to us various principles found in God's Word. When we are wrestling with an issue, after my wife and I have discussed and prayed about it we turn to our son and his wife for their counsel, instruction, and even correction. We relate to each other as peers now because he is no longer under our authority.

Children must accept responsibility for making their own decisions. Leaving mother and father means that people must put off the inordinate need for their parents' approval and the thoughtless tendency to imitate their parents out of habit. Children ought to replace their unthinking and obsessive dependence with the practice of examining all of their choices and the practices and ideas of their parents against the teaching of God's Word.

After marriage, it is still proper for people to seek the counsel of their parents. Now, however, the mothers and fathers should be regarded and respected as advisors and resources of wisdom rather than as authority figures. The decisions of a married couple should be based on what they have personally discovered from God's Word and godly counselors, not simply on what their parents want. Leaving means that people learn to look at their parents objectively, evaluate their strengths and weaknesses, and love them anyway because God has given their mothers and fathers to them.

Children must put on the willingness to honestly and respectfully discuss their family backgrounds with their mates without becoming defensive. As we have already noted, family history has an impact on people as adults and on their expectations in marriage. When I do premarital counseling, I do a Family of Origin Study with the couple so that they have the opportunity to work through and evaluate their family backgrounds together. Taking some time to do this before marriage helps young people avoid major problems later because they already know about and have dealt with some of the things that can cause friction. (I encourage you to complete the Family of Origin Study[3] included in appendix 2 to get the maximum benefit out of this booklet.)

Children must put on the determination to make their mate, rather than their parents or anyone else, the most significant human being in their lives. Scripture is very clear on this matter in many passages with one of them being Ephesians 5:22–33:

> Wives, be subject to *your own husband, as* to the Lord. . . . *as* the church is subject to Christ, so also the wives ought to be *to their husbands in everything.* Husbands, *love your wives just as* Christ also loved the church . . . . So husbands ought also to *love their own wives as* their own bodies. He who *loves his own wife* loves himself; for no one ever hated his own flesh, but nourishes and cherishes it, just *as* Christ also does the church . . . . each individual among you also is to *love his own wife* even *as* himself, and the wife must see to it that she respects [reverences, admires] her husband.

As you read this passage, don't miss the point that it is making by using the word "*as*" six times. Two times God indicates that the way a wife relates to her husband is be similar to the way believers are to relate to the Lord. The other four times discuss the way a husband is to relate to his wife, comparing it to how the Lord cares for the church and the way a man cares for himself. What stronger words could our Lord have used to emphasize that the marital relationship must be *the most significant human relationship*? Personally, I can't think of any way that God could have made the fact clearer than He did here. That, I'm convinced, is part and parcel of what leaving mother and father involves.

3. Wayne A. Mack, *Preparing for Marriage God's Way* (Tulsa: Hensley, 1996), 33.

Children must be prepared to give their mate's parents the same respect and honor they give their own parents. When two people get married, they each gain a new set of parents—that is part of becoming one flesh. As they put off the exclusive parent-child relationship that they had with their own parents, they must at the same time work at putting on a proper and appropriate peer relationship with both sets of parents that places them on equal footing.

Leaving father and mother as God intends is not a simple thing to do. It involves consciously doing many things that will help us to develop the type of relationship that God desires adult children to have with their parents. It is vitally important, however, that we be diligent about fulfilling God's first command to married people (Gen. 2:24). God, who is the Author of marriage, knew from the beginning that the issue of leaving parents would be crucial to the success of the marriage relationship.

Practical Guidelines for Leaving

How do we successfully implement the leaving process after we get married?

First, I always tell young people that they must not allow their parents to demean their mate. If a mother, for example, accuses her son-in-law of some wrongdoing, her daughter has a responsibility to respond by saying something like this: "Mother, I love you, but God says I am to revere and respect my husband (Eph. 5:33; Prov. 31:10–12). If you have a problem with something he has done, you need to talk to him about it privately, as the Bible commands"(Matt. 18:15). On the other hand, husbands and wives must be very careful to avoid complaining to their parents about their spouses as this can make it difficult for parents to love and respect their child's spouse as they should. In all things regarding their parents, husbands and wives should talk together and make mutual decisions about how they—as one flesh—will relate to them.

Second, we should always look for ways to commend and build up our mate to our parents. This means that, without being dishonest, we should look for every opportunity to extol our mate's virtues and avoid talking about negative things to our parents. Since our parents know us best and our mate least, they will get much of their opinion and regard for our mate from what they hear us say. To the extent that we are able, it is our responsibility to see that their love and respect for our mate grows over time.

Third, we should always make an effort to be sure that our mate feels included in family discussions and activities. Sometimes, without even realizing it, mates are treated as outsiders when families get together. I have seen this happen on a number of occasions. The in-law is ignored in the conversation, which often revolves around "inside" family information. Being one flesh means that husbands and wives should function as a team in all things. This may require a special effort on the part of the biological child to make sure their spouse is included.

Fourth, it is important for husbands and wives to choose a course of action together when problems arise with a parent. Whatever the issue, it should be first taken before the Lord in prayer and, if appropriate, counsel from another person may be sought out. When we've decided how to handle the situation, we ought to respectfully go to our parents and discuss it with them. If they disagree with us, we must also be ready to handle the conflict in a mature way, allowing them the right to their own opinion. Unless we are able to put these things into practice, we will still be functioning as children who have not left our parents.

Because I know that properly leaving mother and father is a crucial factor for developing God's kind of marriage, I always discuss this aspect of marriage when I do premarital counseling. I am convinced the leaving prescribed in Genesis 2:24 is so important that I devote a whole section to it in the premarital counseling manual I developed, *Preparing for Marriage God's Way.* In one of the assignments in that section each person is asked to write a letter to his or her parents (which may or may not actually be given to them) describing their views of how they think God would have children and parents relate to each other after children are married. To help them in accomplishing this task, the couple is instructed to adapt and alter a sample letter describing what I consider to be a biblical portrayal of what this relationship should look like. I quote it at this point because I think it gives a clear and practical representation of what it means to leave mother and father. I encourage all married people who are reading this booklet to reflect on what it says and use it for evaluative, instructional, and corrective purposes.

Dear Mom and Dad,

I want to thank you for your love and devotion to me as I was growing up. You have been good parents, bringing me up in the instruction and discipline of the Lord. You have been used of God to make me what I am. Through you, your words, your actions, reactions and attitudes, I have learned. To you I am deeply indebted and grateful and will always be.

At this time, a very important time in each of our lives, our relationship will change—not deteriorate, but change. Scriptures assert that for the cause of marriage men and women shall leave their mothers and fathers. Well, that time has arrived in my life. As a Christian I will always honor you, appreciate you, respect you, pray for you, commend you and seek to help you, but still God says I must leave. And in obedience to the Lord I will do that.

God says that next to my relationship to Him—or perhaps I should say as part of my relationship to Him—my relationship with my wife/husband must become the priority relationship in life. I am sure you will agree.

From the time of our wedding onward _____ and I will become one flesh. We want to have the relationship God intends and to be everything that God wants us to be. I ask you to regard _____ as a part of the family in the same way as you regard me. After all, the Bible says we have become one flesh and he who loves his wife/husband, loves himself/herself. I ask you to help us learn how to practically merge our two independent lives into a one-flesh relationship practically.

You have been given wisdom from God and from time to time, we will be turning to you for counsel. When we do, we will take your counsel seriously, but under God we will think, search the Scriptures and pray, and determine God's will for ourselves. We want and need your continued love and assistance, but God has called us to establish a new family for Christ, developing our own unique lifestyle within the framework of Scripture. We want to be your friends as well as your children. We want you to be free to agree or disagree with us and love us regardless. We want the same freedom. This will be hard for us and for you. After all, up to this point under God you have been my number one authority in life under God. I have come to depend on you, to look first to you for counsel and support and assistance. Now that changes, and change is hard, for me and for you.

Please understand what I am saying—I/we want to be what God wants. I/we want our relationship with you to be a good one. I/we love you deeply, respect you greatly, and are expecting that the future will bring new and enjoyable aspects to our relationship. Thanks again for all you are and have been to us. I/ we love you.

Son/Daughter[4]

(Completing the inventory in appendix 3 will be useful in helping you to evaluate how well you are fulfilling this aspect of God's plan for parent-child relations after marriage.)

The Parents' Side of Leaving

Earlier we considered the issue of what it means for couples to leave mother and father. Then we drew out some of the

4. Mack, Preparing, 33.

practical implications for actually accomplishing this important biblical directive.

In this section I want to discuss the flip side of the leaving endeavor by suggesting some practical guidelines for parents whose children have married and have left the home. These guidelines, when followed, can be very helpful in smoothing out the biblically commanded leaving process for married children.

Remember the passage in Genesis 2:24: "For this reason a man shall leave his father and his mother, and be joined to his wife; and they shall become one flesh." I think it is quite interesting that God made this statement about leaving father and mother to a couple who didn't have children or parents! What was His intention in giving Adam and Eve a directive that they could not immediately put into practice? I believe that God made this statement to them because He knew that they were going to have children and it would be their responsibility to teach them about marriage. It would be important for Adam and Eve as the first parents both to model a godly marriage relationship and to allow and encourage their children to leave them and establish their own families.

First, parents must make sure that the primary human relationship in their lives is with their spouse. This must be true both before and after children have left home.

Second, as parents raise their children, they should prepare themselves for the time when they will leave them. I have counseled women who became depressed when the last child left the house. They were so wrapped up in the lives of their children that their purpose and meaning left when the children did. This occurred because they had not properly prepared themselves for this eventuality.

Third, parents must prepare and train their children for leaving. As our children grow older, they should be expected to take on more and more responsibility for their decisions and actions. Parents who make all the decisions for their children effectively cripple them. As a rule, parents should try not to make decisions for their children that their children are capable of making. Instead of stepping in, parents should teach them *how* to make decisions. Even when children are young, we should use every opportunity to teach them biblical principles for decision making.

Years ago, when we were living in Louisiana, one of my sons announced that he wanted to buy a dirt bike. Apparently, many of the other boys he knew were getting them and he wanted one too. So I said to him, "Okay, how are you going to make a decision as to whether or not you are going to buy a dirt bike?" I did not say yes or no to him because it seemed to be a good opportunity to teach him about decision making.

I told my son that he and I both needed to consider this question. I also reminded him that I always wanted him to do everything to the glory of God, as 1 Corinthians 10:31 commands. I explained that whenever I have a decision to make, I will evaluate the situation—small and large alike—in terms of whether or not it will help me glorify God. I asked him to think about whether his owning a dirt bike would meet that criterion. In order to get him to think through this issue carefully and effectively, I asked him to make a list of ways that a dirt bike might help or hinder him from glorifying God. I wanted him to gather information and think through it properly before he made a decision. After making his list, he came back to me and said, "Dad, after thinking about it, I've decided that I shouldn't get a dirt bike." Without ever having to tell him no—and I probably would not have—I was able to help him make a decision not based on feelings but on godly principles. Rather than making wise decisions for our children, we must teach them to do it for themselves.

Fourth, parents must always keep in mind that their children have been loaned to them by God. They are not our property. "Behold, children are a gift of the LORD, the fruit of the womb is a reward" (Ps. 127:3). Every time we look at our children, we ought to remind ourselves that they do not belong to us. There would be far less child abuse in this world if more parents really understood the fact that their children belong to God and they are not entitled to them or anything from them. Because they are only on loan to us, our relationship with them must change dramatically when they marry or reach a marrying age.

Fifth, as parents raise their children, they must be careful to give them the right to respectfully disagree without being hurt or angry with them and without punishing them. On issues where there is no clear "Thus saith the Lord," parents should allow their children the right to disagree with them, and even if there is a clear commandment, they can allow them to disagree and then teach them why they are wrong without being overbearing or nasty. Parents ought to take these opportunities to help their children grow in wisdom, both by prayer and by demonstration.

For example, when one child wrongs another, parents should explain to him that he has sinned against God and against his brother or sister. Because of this, he ought to pray and ask God for forgiveness and ask his sibling for forgiveness as well. I do not, however, believe that it is of any value to force the offending child (prematurely) to go through the charade of saying he is sorry when he really is not. If he is not sorry, it is an indication that he has not reached the point of even understanding or admitting that what he did was wrong. Helping him grow in wisdom regarding his sin is far more important (and difficult) than simply forcing an obligatory "I'm sorry" out of him.

Sixth, parents should help their children leave by accepting their child's mate as an equal to their own child. In other words, they should not be thinking about "my daughter" and "my son-in-law" in different categories of love and respect. When our children get married, our family grows and we must be willing to love, respect, and treat that new child as an equal to our own. I have no less regard for my daughters-in-law than I do my own daughter, and Lord willing, when my daughter gets married, by God's grace, I will grant to her husband the same regard that I do my own sons, recognizing them as one flesh. Understanding that they are no longer separate individuals but rather a unit, I know that showing respect for my daughter will require respecting her husband.

Seventh, parents ought to seek to develop a proper peer relationship with their adult children. This means that parents should influence their adult children primarily by example, and when necessary and biblically appropriate, through gentle, humble, and well-timed verbal counsel and advice. Parents should make it easy and desirable for their adult children to receive their perspectives on the issues they are facing. When older children do something that parents think is unbiblical, they ought to make every effort to make their lives a model of the truth that their children are failing to observe. When biblical counsel is clearly needed, parents ought to make every effort to approach them in a "follow us as we follow Christ" manner. They ought to make sure that the counsel or admonition they give is really based on Scripture and not just their preferences and opinions (Isa. 8:20; Luke 17:3; 1 John 3:4).

Before seeking to instruct or correct children in any area of life, parents should seriously pray that God would prepare them to receive and give counsel in a truly biblical manner (Col. 4:2–3). Before they instruct or correct, they should consider how to answer rather than just blurt out whatever comes to mind (Prov. 15:28). They should make sure that their counsel is in keeping with Ephesians 4:29, which admonishes us to speak only that which is good according to the need of the moment and for the purpose of edification, ministering grace, and help to our adult children. Properly relating to adult children involves using sweetness of speech and wisdom to make knowledge acceptable (Prov. 15:2; 16:21).

As parents attempt to influence their adult children, they must use soft speech rather than hard, irritable words (Prov. 25:15); they must appeal and persuade rather than demand and push. Parents must also determine whether the issue they are addressing is actually a sinful pattern and not one of those things that Scripture says should be overlooked (Prov. 19:11; Luke 17:3; Gal. 6:1).

Eighth, parents should be careful not to do anything, such as criticize or nag, that would weaken their children's marriage relationship. Instead, they ought to look for every opportunity to praise and encourage their child's spouse. It also means they should be careful not to abuse the hospitality of their children just as they would with their friends. Parents should have the same respect for their children's privacy as they do for anyone else they know. In all things, they should act toward them with unconditional and unselfish love, never expecting or demanding anything in return. Helping children to properly leave at the appropriate time is an important part of keeping the marriage relationship a priority as God intended for both parents and children.

(Complete the In-Law Inventory for Parents in appendix 4 as an aid for evaluating and promoting the leaving aspect from the parent's perspective.)

Other Types of Leaving

Leaving father and mother is an important part of establishing and maintaining a godly marriage. There are, however, other types of leaving that must take place in order for marriage to be the priority that God desires it to be. In 1 Corinthians 7:33–34, Paul implies that marriage requires some major changes to our focus in life. By discussing the things that single people are free to do for the Lord, he intimates that married people have to be focused largely on their relationship to each other.

When we get married, we must leave behind anything that will keep us from becoming totally one with our spouse. One of these things is our previous identification as a single person. We have to train ourselves to start thinking and talking in terms of "we" and "us" instead of "I" and "me." When married people fail to do this, it is an indication that they are still trying to carve out a niche for themselves as an individual. If marriage is our chief priority, we have to leave behind our independence in all things—time, money, friendships, desires, work, recreation, and the like. There is no room for "only me" in "one flesh."

Lastly, you and your spouse need to discuss whether or not your marriage is the priority that it ought to be and how to make improvements and changes that are needed. Good communication is crucial to a meaningful relationship. Studying the things I've previously mentioned is a good first step, but it is only a first step. Following God's blueprint for marriage involves much effort, but the reward—a happy and secure marriage that lasts a lifetime—is far greater.

(Completing the assignments in appendixes 1 and 5 will help you evaluate how well you are fulfilling this aspect of leaving in God's plan for parent-child relations after marriage. Studying and following the procedures outlined in appendix 6 will provide a biblical way of handling and potentially resolving any in-law problems you may have.)

Appendix 1: Application and Discussion Exercises

1. Review this booklet and list everything it includes about the putting off aspect of leaving.

2. Have you ever had a conflict with your mate because of the way that either of you were relating to your parents or in-laws?

3. How is it possible to remain tied to your parents in an unbiblical way even after they have died or you have moved many miles away?

4. Have either of you ever thought that your mate was more devoted to and concerned about his or her parents than about you?

5. Evaluate yourself and your mate in terms of how well you have accomplished the putting off aspects of leaving. Use the rating scale: excellent, couldn't be better—4; good, but needs a little fine-tuning—3; fair, needs some changes—2; poor, needs a lot of changes—1; terrible, couldn't be worse—0.

6. Are there ways in which you need to make some changes in the putting off aspect of leaving? What are they?

7. What can you do to improve your relationship with your mate by changing the way you relate to your parents or in-laws?

8. Review this booklet and list everything it includes about the putting on aspect of leaving.

9. Have you ever had a conflict with your mate because you thought that the other person was not putting on any of the things mentioned in this booklet?

10. What does and doesn't it mean to have a peer relationship with your parents? What would and wouldn't be true in a peer relationship?

11. Evaluate yourself and your mate in terms of how well you have accomplished the putting on aspects of leaving described in this booklet. Use the rating scale: excellent, couldn't be better—4; good, but needs a little fine-tuning—3; fair, needs some changes—2; poor, needs a lot of changes—1; terrible, couldn't be worse—0.

12. Are there ways in which you need to make some changes in the putting on aspect of leaving? What are they?

13. What can you do to improve your relationship with your mate by changing the putting on aspects of the way you relate to your parents or in-laws?

14. Think of all the ways your families of origin are alike and all the ways they are different. (See appendix 2 for help in doing this assignment.)

15. Discuss how the similarities have been of help to your relationship.

16. Discuss how the differences may have caused difficulties in your relationship.

17. Identify what these verses teach about how marriage changes parent-child relationships.

    Genesis 2:24–25

    Mark 3:31–35

    Luke 2:41–45

    John 2:1–5

18. Identify what these same verses teach about continuing parent-child responsibilities after marriage occurs.

19. What is the scriptural basis for saying that after your relationship with God, your marriage should be the preeminent relationship in your life?

20. Study Genesis 29–32 and note everything you can about the relationship that Jacob had with his father-in-law, Laban. How would you describe this relationship? What do you notice about the way Jacob treated his father-in-law? What do you notice about the way Laban treated his son-in-law? Would you say that this was a good relationship? Why or why not?

21. Study Exodus 18:1–27 and notice how Moses and his father-in-law Jethro related to one another. How would you describe this relationship? What do you notice about the way Moses treated his father-in-law? What do you notice about the way Jethro treated his son-in-law? Would you say that this was a good relationship? Why or why not?

22. What is meant by this booklet's argument indicating that leaving father and mother involves more than most people realize?

23. What are the common mistakes that in-laws (children and parents, brothers-in-law, sisters-in-law, etc.) make?

24. What advice would you give to someone about the way that married people should relate to their parents or in-laws?

25. What should and should not characterize the relationship of married people with their parents or in-laws?

Now that you have read this booklet and done the application questions, move on to complete the assignments in appendixes 2–5.

Appendix 2: Family of Origin Study

DISCUSS TOGETHER the similarities and differences between your families and write down your findings. Make sure you discuss the following items and evaluate how these similarities and differences have affected you personally and how they may affect your marriage relationship.[1]

1. Family occupations—blue collar versus white collar, both parents work or just one works, etc.

2. The quality of your parents' marriages—good, fair, poor, still together, divorced, separated, many conflicts, good communication, enjoyed being together, etc.

3. Family rules—for example, clearly stated versus unstated but implied, many rules versus few rules, etc. What were the rules by which your family operated?

4. Personality features and characteristics of mother and father.

5. Family beliefs—about God, church, Christ, salvation, the Bible, the purpose of life, etc.

1. Mack, *Preparing*, 30.

6. Views about money—frugal versus wasteful, its importance, how to spend, savings, who makes decisions, etc.

7. Views about sex—discussed freely, never discussed, what has been said or implied.

8. Views about responsibilities and roles of husband/father and wife/mother—who does what, who makes decisions, who really leads the family, etc.

9. Relationship with extended family—how close, how frequently visited, how they are viewed, how much time spent with them, how important, etc.

10. Involvement in church activities and spiritual things—devotions, attendance at church, overall involvement, giving to church, etc.

11. Family political views.

12. Views about work, recreation, and vacations.

13. Family secrets—Dad has a bad temper, Mom is very emotional, etc.

14. Ways of handling problems, disagreements, ways of communicating, ways of making decisions, etc.

15. Family values and standards—spoken and unspoken values, pretended versus real values, what was considered to be good and bad behavior, good and bad manners, etc.

16. Family boundaries—personal privacy issues, ideas about personal possessions, freedom to disagree and be an individual, liberty to have individual interests and to make decisions, extent to which other people were allowed into family affairs, expressions of affection, attitudes toward fun and recreation, etc.

Summary Questions

1. How are your family backgrounds similar and different?

2. How are your mothers and fathers alike or different?

3. How are you like your father? How are you like your mother?

4. In what ways do you function in marriage and are you inclined to function in marriage as your mother and father did?

5. How is your marriage different (or going to be different if you are not already married) from the marriage of your mother and father?

6. What impact has your family background had or could have on you personally and on your marriage relationship, both positively and negatively?

Appendix 3: In-Law Inventory for Adult Children

THIS INVENTORY is designed for couples to evaluate how they are doing in terms of their relationship with their parents.[1]

Rating Scale: 0 = not at all; 1 = some; 2 = very much

		You	Mate
1.	Excessive dependence on parents	_____	_____
2.	Jealous of mate's relationship with parents	_____	_____
3.	Critical of mate's parents or relatives	_____	_____
4.	Gossips to parents about mate	_____	_____
5.	Critical of mate to parents	_____	_____
6.	Takes sides with parents against mate	_____	_____
7.	Excessive talking about parents	_____	_____
8.	Compares mate with parents	_____	_____
9.	Demonstrates partiality to own parents	_____	_____
10.	Puts parents above mate	_____	_____

1. Mack, *Preparing*, 34.

11. Favorably compares your own
    parents with mate's parents   _____   _____

12. Makes plans with parents without
    seeking mate's counsel or opinion   _____   _____

13. Allows parents to dominate   _____   _____

14. Frequently boasts about own parents _____   _____

15. Excessive desire to please parents   _____   _____

16. Bitter toward parents or mate's parents _____   _____

17. Indifferent toward parents or mate's
    parents   _____   _____

18. Relationship with own parents has
    caused problems in marriage   _____   _____

19. Mate's relationship with own parents
    has caused problems in marriage   _____   _____

Appendix 4:
In-Law Inventory
for Parents

THIS INVENTORY is designed for parents to evaluate how they are doing in terms of their relationship with their adult married children.[1]

Rating Scale: 0 = not at all; 1 = some; 2 = very much

	You	Mate
1. Find fault with child	____	____
2. Find fault with child's mate	____	____
3. Meddle in child's affairs/marriage	____	____
4. Have unrealistic expectations of post-marriage relationship with child	____	____
5. Have unbiblical, unrealistic expectations of child's mate	____	____
6. Make unbiblical, unrealistic demands on child	____	____

1. Mack, *Preparing*, 35.

7. Make unbiblical demands on child's mate _____ _____

8. Are overly possessive or protective of child _____ _____

9. Are aloof or indifferent toward child _____ _____

10. Are aloof or indifferent toward child's mate _____ _____

11. Are overly dependent on child after marriage _____ _____

12. Gossip about child or child's mate _____ _____

13. Insist on having your own way with child _____ _____

14. Talk too much about child or child's mate _____ _____

15. Are jealous of child's mate _____ _____

16. Won't listen to child or child's mate _____ _____

17. Are unappreciative of child or child's mate _____ _____

18. Are bitter toward child or child's mate _____ _____

19. Are jealous of other set of parents _____ _____

20. Are jealous of child's relationship with other people _____ _____

21. Give opinions too freely _____ _____

Appendix 5: How Are We Doing?

TAKE SOME TIME to think through the following questions as a means of evaluating how you are doing in the area of leaving. Then, after you make your evaluation, ask your spouse for his or her perspective on each of these questions and have your spouse give you his or her reasons for answering as they did. Make sure you listen without interruption, without defensiveness, without excuse making, and without arguing. Just listen and learn all you can about your mate's perspective and then seek to change in whatever way would be in keeping with God's will for your marriage relationship.

1. Who means more to me: my spouse, my children, my parents, or my friends?

2. What means more to me: talking with my spouse or talking with someone else?

3. What means more to me: my spouse's opinion or someone else's opinion?

4. What means more to me: meeting my own desires or meeting the desires of my spouse?

5. Which would I rather do: pray with my spouse or pray in church/at Bible study/by myself?

6. What means more to me: spending time with my spouse or at work/hobbies/church activities?

7. What means more to me: the respect and appreciation of my spouse or that of my boss, parents, friends, or others?

8. What means more to me: my spouse's displeasure or disapproval or that of someone else?

9. In addition to thinking through these questions, I suggest that you seek out other resources for improving your marriage. Here are some good books on the subject: *Sweethearts for a Lifetime* (by Wayne and Carol Mack), *Strengthening Your Marriage* (by Wayne Mack), *Your Family God's Way* (by Wayne Mack), *Christian Living in the Home* (by Jay Adams), *A Homework Manual for Biblical Living: Family and Marital Problems* (by Wayne Mack), *The Home Beautiful* (by J. R. Miller). Proverbs 15:10 says, "He who hates reproof will die," so it is important that we constantly search for ways to be corrected if we want to keep our marriage relationship alive and healthy.

Appendix 6:
Practical Considerations for
Resolving In-Law Conflicts

Lou Priolo

BIBLICAL COUNSELORS are often called upon to help people resolve interpersonal relationships between in-laws. After reading this booklet, this should be no surprise to you. The question you may have at this point is, "How is this done?"

In this appendix, I would like to give a suggested procedure that I trust you will find helpful in resolving conflicts with your in-laws. Admittedly, some conflicts are very complex—typically because of the manipulative tendencies of one or more of the individuals involved.[1] These usually require the assistance of a mediator—a true "yokefellow" (Phil. 4:3 NIV) who can serve as a peacemaker between parties. Of course, as a rule, it is good to seek godly counsel even when attempting to resolve conflicts in house. As I often tell those I counsel, "There is usually more than one way to skin a cat biblically." Keep in mind that what I am suggesting is not the only (and not necessarily the best) way to resolve all in-law issues. But if you don't have a better

---

1. If you believe you are dealing with manipulative individuals, you might want to consider reading my booklet in this Resources for Changing Lives series titled *Manipulation: Knowing How to Respond.*

option, you might want to consider this approach (or a modified version of it).

The first step is *being committed to living at peace with your in-laws/parents as much as it depends on you*. God doesn't want there to be any loose ends between Christians that have not been tied up. Indeed, He tells us to "make every effort to keep the unity of the Spirit through the bond of peace" (Eph. 4:3 NIV). We are to "seek peace and pursue it" (1 Peter 3:11).

"But what if my in-laws are not believers?" God wants us to pursue peace with all kinds of people—even unbelievers. Hebrews 12:14 commands believers to "pursue peace with all men." Likewise, Romans 12:18 urges us, "If possible, so far as it depends on you, be at peace with all men." "All men" includes unbelievers.

The first stipulation of this verse is a *conditional* one, "*If possible* . . . be at peace with all men" (believers and unbelievers). It is not always possible for Christians to be at peace with unbelievers–even in marriage (cf. 1 Cor. 7:15). But, there is no reason why two *believers* cannot learn how to be at peace with one another. The second stipulation is *unconditional*, "*so far as it depends on you*, be at peace with all men." You must pursue peace with all men *regardless* of their response to you. Your obedience to God does not depend on the response of others. Your love for your neighbor (or enemy for that matter) should not be conditional (in that it is not predicated on his love for you). Regardless of your in-law's willingness to be at peace with you, *you* should be willing (to initiate and pursue) to be at peace with him—especially if he is a fellow believer.

If an in-law or parent is not at peace with you, it may be (at least in part) the fruit of your sinful behavior. Let me suggest in the form of three questions[2] some reasons why there may not be peace between you.

---

2. These questions have been adapted from Jay E. Adams, *How to Overcome Evil* (Phillipsburg, NJ: P&R Publishing, 1977).

1. Have I *provoked* him to evil? Your in-law's/parent's contention with you may, in part, be a sinful response to an evil that you have first committed against him. While he is not thereby exonerated, you are required to seek his forgiveness for any sin you may have committed that provoked him to evil in the first place.

2. Have I *protracted* (aggravated) his evil by a sinful response in return? Is it possible that rather than responding with good to his sin, you responded in kind (perhaps with even more evil than he inflicted against you) and that such a sinful response on your part has contributed greatly to the lack of peace between you?

3. Have I *prolonged* the problem by not dealing with it quickly? Conflicts between believers are to be resolved expeditiously. "Therefore if you are presenting your offering at the altar, and there remember that your brother has something against you, leave your offering there before the altar, and go; first be reconciled to your brother, and then come and present your offering" (Matt. 5:23–24). The longer you wait to resolve conflicts, the more bitterness and suspicion can take root and fester.

This leads us to the second step in the reconciliation process: *get the beam out of your own eye first.*

> Why do you look at the speck that is in your brother's eye, but do not notice the log that is in your own eye? Or how can you say to your brother, "Let me take the speck out of your eye," and behold, the log is in your own eye? You hypocrite, first take the log out of your own eye, and then you will see clearly to take the speck out of your brother's eye. (Matt. 7: 3–5)

Humility begets humility. I cannot emphasize this enough. I have learned the hard way never to allow those I counsel to enter such reconciliation meetings without thoroughly preparing them to first "take the hit" for their own sins. By humbling yourself in the eyes of your in-laws, you may set the tone for the entire conversation. More importantly, as a Christian, you should always maintain a clear conscience not only before God, but also before man. "I also do my best to maintain always a blameless conscience *both* before God and before men" (Acts 24:16; cf. 23:1; 2 Cor. 1:12; 1 Tim. 1:5; 3:9; 2 Tim. 1:13; Heb. 13:18).

This means that you will not only have to confess your sins to your in-laws/parents but will also have to sincerely seek their forgiveness. I can think of no better way to prepare for this than by utilizing Wayne's In-Law Inventory for Adult Children (appendix 3). Put yourself in their places. Try to see your offenses through their eyes. Prepare a list that you can recite to them in the process of humbly asking their forgiveness.

The third step is to *write out a sort of declaration of independence from your parents.* Using the letter Wayne has provided on pages 22–23 as a template, construct your own personalized letter that you can read to them (and perhaps give to them) at the time of your meeting. Consider whether to include items (positively stated)[3] from the In-Law Inventory for Parents (appendix 4). In most cases, after reading the letter, it would be proper to offer to discuss with them the details of its content.

This raises the question, "Should we try to convict them of their pattern of sin and press them to seek our forgiveness?" If your in-laws are professing Christians, Luke 17:3 is a passage you should consider: "Take heed to yourselves. If your brother sins against you, rebuke him; and if he repents, forgive him" (NKJV). Jesus says that for personal offenses that cannot be covered in love (1 Peter 4:8) or overlooked (Prov.

3. For example, rather than saying, "You must stop finding fault with _____," you might say, "We ask that you look for ways to commend _____." Instead of saying, "Please don't meddle in our affairs," you might try, "We ask that from this time forward you commit to respecting our privacy" (or "one flesh relationship").

19:11), believers are to convict (reprove) each other. That is, we are to humbly and gently go to our brother with the intent of getting him to see and acknowledge his sin so that we might grant him forgiveness.

Another thing to do before attempting to sit down for a reconciliation conference is to *spend time in prayer.* Thank God for the in-law trial into which He has placed you. "Count it all joy" (James 1:2 NKJV). Confess to Him your contribution to the problem. Ask that He would convict you further of any contributions to the problem to which you are still blind. Pray that He would prepare the hearts of your in-laws/parents to want to live in peace with you. Pray for wisdom and grace and for the prerequisite qualities for maintaining unity found in Ephesians 4:2—humility, gentleness, patience, and forbearance.

Once these prerequisites have been completed, the fourth step is to *request a meeting with your in-laws/parents.* The invitation should probably come from the husband as the head of the home. He should also be prepared to facilitate (lead) the meeting. I recommend setting aside no less than 90 minutes, even though the meeting might take much less time than that.

An optional fifth step is to *consider asking your in-laws/parents to read this booklet.* This is a judgment call you will have to make based on your knowledge of them and their receptivity to biblical truth. If you choose to ask them, you can do so before or after your meeting.

Finally, you may have *to accept the fact that some in-law conflicts may not be resolved satisfactorily* because some parties are unwilling to play by God's rules for interpersonal relationships. Although following biblical directives often produces the desired result (peace in this case), sometimes such attempts at reconciliation result in a further alienation. The assurance you want to have in your heart is that, as much as it depends on you, you have done what you could to have a good relationship with them. The point you want to make to them as politely as possible is this: "If we cannot achieve reconciliation, it will not be because I am unwilling to live at peace with you, but rather because you are unwilling to play by God's rules."

May God bless you as you endeavor to be the peacemaker in this and all of your other conflicts.